Dogs Have Souls Too

The Spirit of Miss Sarah

Dogs Have Souls Too

The Spirit of Miss Sarah

GEORGE & EMILY WATSON

PMD PUBLISHING
P.O. BOX 5 2 0 1 5 7
SALT LAKE CITY, UTAH 8 4 1 5 2

DOGS HAVE SOULS TOO
The Spirit of Miss Sarah

Watson, George & Emily
DOGS HAVE SOULS TOO
The Spirit of Miss Sarah – 1 st ed.
Library of Congress Catalog Card Number: 99-91035
ISBN: 0-9674875-0-1

This book is a work of fiction. Names and characters either are products of the author's imagination or are used fictitiously. Any resemblance to actual events or persons, living or dead, is entirely coincidental.

DOGS HAVE SOULS TOO – The Spirit of Miss Sarah is available from your local bookstore or direct from the publisher.

Printed and bound
in the
United States of America

Cover design Robert White

"A Charming gem of a book about love and faith and the enduring spirit of a beloved animal companion. Miss Sarah is surely wagging her tail."

Judith Reitman
Author, Stolen for Profit

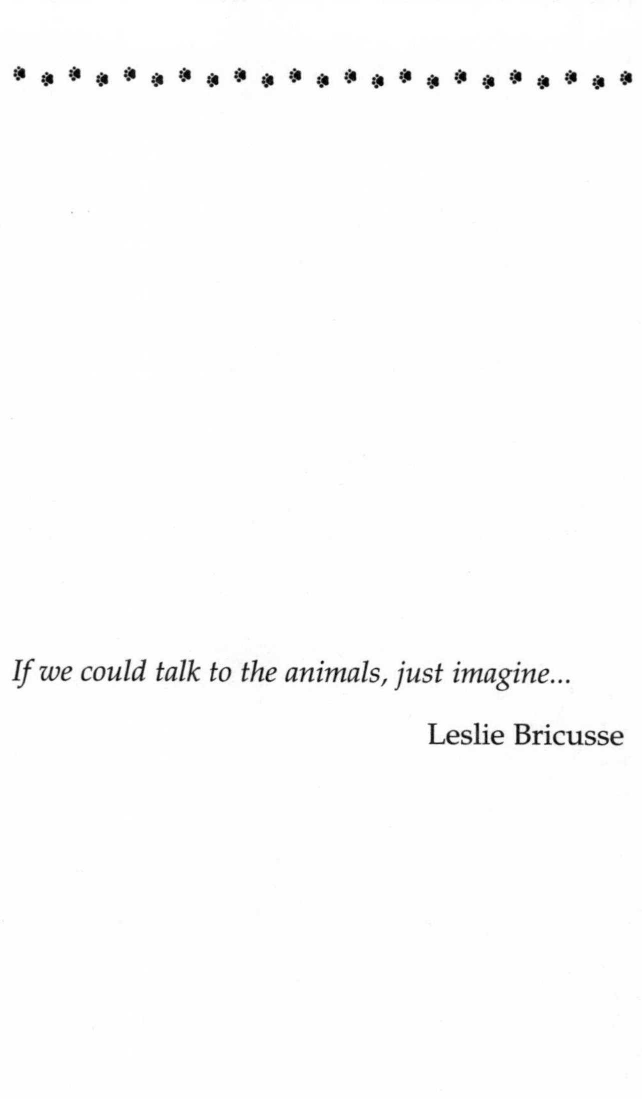

If we could talk to the animals, just imagine...

Leslie Bricusse

In Remembrance

You came. You left. We will always remember.

CHAPTERS

PREFACE

For years, churches worldwide have celebrated the blessing of animals on the feast day of St. Francis of Assisi; nevertheless, churches presently offer little comfort to grieving owners of dying or dead pets.

As pets fill our human need for unconditional love, we exalt their life, and at death, our grief is intense. In the absence of spiritual leadership there is a need for each of us to share our stories, to uplift one another. One way to do this is through stories about dreams; because, having dreams of our animals can be reassuring and spiritually healing. In *DOGS HAVE SOULS TOO*, the reader can reminiscence through the writers' anecdotes of the life they shared with their dog, all the way to death's door and the dream beyond.

Throughout Miss Sarah's story it is easy to see lessons on friendship, patience and unconditional love unfold. Her story also deals with the most difficult issue of all, the one different from the story of man -- Euthanasia. Readers will relate to the nagging, heart wrenching question: When is it time to put my pet to sleep? *DOGS HAVE SOULS TOO* will make readers cry, it will make them laugh, but more importantly, it will give comfort and hope to those who grieve over the loss of their pet.

CHAPTER I

A dream re – quest

Emily was shaking me, trying to wake me. As she shook me, she kept saying, "George. George. Wake up, George." I rolled over and in a ruffled voice asked her what was wrong and she said, "Nothing's wrong. But I just had a dream about Sarah and it was the most realistic dream I have ever had. Even after I woke up, I had to lay here for several minutes trying to figure out if I was dreaming or if it really happened.

I'm not really sure if Sarah could actually talk or if I was reading her mind or what, but one thing is for certain, I understood every word of what she was saying or thinking. Sarah told me she received our message and that she misses and loves us too and there is no need for us to feel or believe that she needs to forgive us. Her heart had so much love for us."

I could see Emily's excitement mounting as she continued, "George, she wants us to take her ashes to where we run in Memory Grove and spread them over the hillside. She says we will know the exact location when we see it. From this location she can look down on the park and, for all time, watch over the people and their animals as they run the paths and play in the park."

A huge smile filled Emily's face as she

said, "Sarah told me that although she is no longer with us physically, her spirit will always be. Sarah said that, most importantly, she wants us to make arrangements for a park bench to be placed in beautiful Memory Grove." Emily took my shoulders into her hands and shook them ever so gently and still smiling, said, "George! She wants us to invite all animal lovers who have lost their four-legged friends, to sit and reminisce on her bench. She said that she would be there, for them, to help them turn their grieving into a happy remembrance."

It was comforting and appealing for me to hear what Emily had to say about her dream, because we could have closure with Sarah's death and continue to have Sarah as a part of our lives. Even though I questioned whether or not Sarah had actually contacted Emily, Emily's dream, point by point, was so precise and so believable that I was going to support Emily in every way possible to see that her dream became a reality.

The next morning we were both up bright and early. At nine we telephoned the Salt Lake City Parks Department and received permission to place a park bench in Memory Grove. We purchased a beautiful black park bench and made arrangements to have a small tag placed on it reading, "Donated by Miss Sarah." The Parks Department would deliver it to a pre-selected location in five days.

The afternoon of the second day Emily and I went to Memory Grove and walked our regular path. We had gone just a short distance when Emily suddenly stopped, pointed at the hillside in front of her and said, "There! Right there!" "Right there, what?" I asked. "The place," Emily said with emotion. "That's the place Sarah wants us to scatter her ashes." "How do you know?" I questioned. "I don't know how I know, but this is the place."

If Sarah selected this location, I thought, she did so because each season provided its own magic. Early Spring flourished with beautiful green trees, huge blue spruce trees, wild grass, and flowers. Late Autumn, the park would be filled with a matrix of colored leaves to romp and roll in. During the Winter months, trees, softly dusted with snow, would make the grove look like a winter wonderland. From this vantage point Sarah would be able to see the park where a cool stream quietly meandered and where people play with their animals. The area was no doubt the right place for Sarah. We went back to our car and drove straight to the veterinarian's, where we retrieved Sarah's ashes.

We returned to the hillside on the fourth day after Sarah was put to sleep. It only took a few minutes to scatter the fist-sized package of Sarah's ashes along the hillside, which included her incinerated dog tags. On our way back home, Emily was quiet; she had something on her mind. After a few minutes of driving, she said, "George, you know what? I was just thinking. No one is going to believe us when we tell our story." "It really doesn't matter Emily," I assured her, "because in our hearts we both know it's true and so does Sarah. Anyone that uses Sarah's bench, having experienced a loss of a four-legged friend, will soon feel what we have--her comforting power."

The next time we went to Memory Grove, we went with the anticipation of seeing and sitting on Sarah's bench. Little did we know that we would meet and speak to someone Sarah had already touched. The power of her presence was felt again.

CHAPTER II

A stay of execution

My name is Emily. Sarah's story, for me, begins Mother's Day weekend, 1981. I had exhausted all leads to find a Persian Siamese cat for my sister, Barbara, who always had been like a mother to me. There was only one more place to try. The animal shelter.

The cages were filled with fluffy little kittens but none were Persian Siamese. Depressed at not being able to find a special cat for my sister, I wandered through the dog cages thinking of where else to search. As I walked down the isle of cages, dogs were on both sides of me, whining, howling, growling, and pawing at their steel cage doors. Then I saw her. She was sitting in a cage by herself and, unlike the other dogs, she was quiet. Looking a bit matted, the cute, seven-pound, shaggy female terrier just stared at me. As I walked past her cage I kept looking back over my shoulder and saw that she was stretching her neck to look at me. I knew I was not going to leave without her.

I went to the front desk to ask about this adorable little dog. I was told that her name was Sarah and she was a silver hair terrier. She was two years old, fixed, had all of her shots and was dropped off because her owners were moving to a place where they did not allow pets. The staff had kept her days past her time limit and, because she was to be put to sleep that night, they were excited to see that I had an interest in her. Unfortunately, I was new to the area, with a new bank account, and the animal shelter would not accept my check. It was a half hour to closing time and I was an hour from home. I needed to act fast. I searched for a grocery store that would cash my check but three stores later I still did not have the money. I called the animal shelter and begged them not to close and not to put Sarah to sleep. They assured me that they would wait. Desperately, I called a friend who lived nearby. She happily offered to help and, to save time, met me at the shelter to cash my check. For this act of kindness, I am forever grateful because Sarah went home with me.

I was excited about giving Sarah to my sister. I had only the evening to bathe Sarah, put a ribbon around her neck and hide her from Barbara. Tomorrow would be a wonderful Mother's Day.

I was up early the next morning and hardly able to conceal my excitement. With Sarah in my arms I entered Barbara's room and said, "Happy Mother's Day." Her mouth dropped as she said, " She's sooo cute. But I really want a cat. You keep her." I was hurt because she didn't like her present, but as we went through the day, I grew excited about the idea of keeping Sarah. Barbara eventually did get her cat, and Sarah settled in nicely with George and me.

I wouldn't exactly say, "Sarah settled in nicely with Emily and me." I'm George; I should know.

Emily called me at work to tell me she had a surprise waiting for me at MY home. She said I was to be careful not to move anything placed in the kitchen doorway, the one we used to enter my living room, and she refused to tell me what the surprise was. Emily and I were not married at this time. It was my home that she brought her surprise to, and she wanted to give this surprise to me. Because she fell in love with this dog she thought I was duty-bound to do the same. Wrong! At that time, I had no desire to care for any animal and that included, but was not limited to, cats, dogs, sheep, horses, and, yes, women.

Later that day as I entered my home and walked toward my kitchen, I could see a large box placed in the doorway, obviously being used as a barricade. I had forgotten about Emily's surprise. As I walked up to the box, I peeked over and sheepishly looking up at me (and I just said I wanted nothing to do with sheep) was this frightened little dog. I was ... uuh, she was cute. I made a few attempts to get the dog to come to me, but she wanted nothing to do with me. I was sure I wanted nothing to do with her, either. I walked away and left her alone; she gave me the same courtesy.

That evening when Emily arrived, she was excited about her new found love, a love she had rescued from certain death. She pleaded with me to let Sarah stay and told me the story of how she went to the animal shelter to get a cat for her sister and how she saw this dog that was supposed to be put to . . . well, you know the story. I put my foot down: "the dog goes!" I said. Emily said, "the dog stays." Seventeen years later, I'm glad I allowed Emily to keep my dog. I hope no one forgets that Emily brought this dog to my home to give to me as a surprise.

CHAPTER III

George remembers sweet memories

Sarah was a shy pup. She lived with us for three months before I realized she could bark. She tried so hard to please us and never failed in her effort. For the seventeen years we had Sarah, she gave us her unconditional love. She had the sweetest and most expressive eyes I had ever seen. When I would look deep into them I could see the years of wisdom she was able to capture in such a short time. They could brighten the darkest day or melt a heart of stone. Sarah always knew when Emily or I was down. On those rare occasions, she would come up and put her head in our lap and lick our hand, as if to say, "I understand and I'm here for you." She had a way about her that, without reservation, was healing. Just looking at her made us smile. What a picker-upper she was.

I have no idea how it started, but Sarah saw the vacuum as an enemy to be conquered. When anyone brought the vacuum out of the closet and switched it on, Sarah came out of nowhere, charging after it with a vengeance. She would bite, bark, even block the vacuum so it couldn't move. She did whatever was necessary to defend her home, and in each battle she showed her aggression until the vacuum retreated to the closet. With the vacuum safely out of sight, Sarah would end her assault with one last bark. She sure put the fear of Dog into the vacuum.

Whenever and wherever we vacationed, we always took Sarah. She was a terrific travel companion. Regardless of whether she was sleeping or awake, she made us smile. She was so therapeutic. She was at her best when we were in open country. She reminded us of a swift little gazelle with legs stiff, head held high and back bent, gracefully soaring over wild brush as she ran free. We called her Air Sarahdan, after Michael Jordan, because she seemed to defy the law of gravity by hanging in mid-air much longer than we thought possible and then gliding softly back to earth.

Sarah loved being out-of-doors and around water. Bathing was another thing.

At bath time, she did everything she could to prevent us from putting her into the tub. Her little legs were swimming before they touched the water and the moment they touched, it was a fight to keep her there. "Please don't do this to me" she seemed to plead. The moment she was out of the tub she would shake all over us and the bathroom. Then she would head for the living room carpet where she would roll and rub herself dry. Once dry, she would prance around looking for a treat for being so good.

She was completely different when it came to water play. She loved any kind of water: streams, rivers, lakes, it made no difference. On our first fishing trip with Sarah in Enis, Montana, Emily and Sarah lay on a blanket by the car while I fished. Emily decided to see if I had had any luck. I had one rainbow trout about 20 inches long that weighed close to three pounds. It was on a wire fish stringer attached to brush growing along the river bank. As Emily and I chatted, Sarah sprang to action. She was stretched out with her back paws on the bank and her front paws balanced on a wooden board that was blocked from going down stream by a bush. The board was about a foot long, four inches wide, two inches thick and was floating where the stringer was tied. With her body stretched to its maximum and the tail of the fish in her mouth she was pulling the trout out of the water. Every time she pulled, the board submerged and so did her head; but she didn't care, she held on. Emily and I laughed so hard we cried as we watched Sarah fight the fish. We could have stayed there for hours watching her play.

One time, I was fishing a small river in Parley's Canyon just minutes from downtown Salt Lake City. While my little fishing pal and Emily were walking the fields up stream, I was wading through the water downstream. Just ahead of me the river meandered off to the right and I couldn't see the water more than twenty-five or thirty feet ahead. As I approached the spot where I thought a big lunker might lie concealed, I heard a loud splash farther up stream, out of view. I thought, good, there must be some nice fish. A moment later, Sarah came paddling downstream, her head held high, twisting side to side looking for me. She swam right through the fishing hole I had been sneaking up on. As cute as she was, she wrecked fishing hole after fishing hole. I can see still how terrified she was of bath water, yet, she had a passion for jumping into creeks, streams, rivers and lakes.

I remember, too, driving with my arm around Sarah as she sat on the arm rest separating the driver from the passenger, taking in everything that moved. I remember watching, as we drove down the street, Sarah's head hanging out the window, the wind pushing back the fur on her face. I remember seeing Sarah through the window of our airplane and seeing her wondering expression as she rode up the baggage conveyor. I remember the first time I took Sarah to the park; she jumped out of the car window while I was still moving because she saw two large German Shepherds playing. I remember how she would walk on her pillow at night before laying down; she was the wild wolf preparing for sleep by mashing down its bed. I remember Sarah's unconditional love. I remember her sensitivity. I remember her faithfulness. I remember. I remember. I remember . . .

CHAPTER IV

Through the eyes of Sarah

I bet my mom's fur coat that the neighbors thought I had just won the Idaho state lottery, when Emily and George came home at the end of a long day. I was so excited when I heard their car drive up. I would warm up for the big show by running around the house just before I went to the door to greet them. With my hind end raised, legs spread and braced beneath me, mouth open, tongue hanging out and my head braced on my front paws, I waited. When they opened the door I would take off running, nothing but a blur. I was faster than a speeding bullet as I ran wildly throughout the house. I was able to leap small objects in a single bound and dodge, jump and slide through various pieces of furniture. Sometimes I amazed myself at what lengths I would go to show George and Emily how happy I was to see them. They would always, as Clint Eastwood would say, "make my day" because they always laughed and tried to catch me. When I finally tired they would pick me up, rub my head and give me a big hug. It was worth all the energy I put into welcoming them home.

I used to follow Emily into the kitchen. She was always dropping food on the floor and some days she dropped more than others. She wasn't messy, just careless. If I was quick enough, it was mine. Sometimes I would go two or three days without eating my dog food because I was continually grabbing food scraps that had fallen to the floor. Unfortunately, Emily realized her carelessness and forced me to go back to eating my dog food. Ugh! Speaking of eating, Emily would forget that I didn't like vegetables and occasionally, I would find broccoli in my dog bowl. Now, if George Bush had been a dog, I know for sure that no one would have dared put broccoli in his dog bowl. Anyway, I would find the hated vegetable mixed-in with other foods. Boy, what a chore it was to pick those tiny, itsy, bitsy, little green gooky parts out of my dish and place them on the floor in a neat pile.

Cleaning day in this dog's life was never restful. Emily thought she was multi-tasking, but her cleaning process was so fragmented that it was simply unbelievable. Keeping up was exhausting. I followed Emily into the bathroom where she would start cleaning. No sooner had I curled up on the floor and made myself comfortable when she would go to the kitchen for additional cleaning materials. I would arrive only to discover that she was distracted by something she felt needed cleaning in the kitchen. Thinking she would stay awhile, I would settle in on the throw rug close to the sink and watch. As soon as I was comfortable Emily again would stop what she was doing (notice I didn't say, "finish") and head downstairs to the laundry room to put a load of clothes in the washer. Knowing this would take time, I dutifully followed, and, again, sat waiting for her to finish. When she was ready to go I led the way up the stairs, racing ahead of her.

I never had a chance to settle down. Emily would walk from one room to another and then back to the first room and then back to the other. She had me going in circles. I wasn't trying to protect Emily, I followed her because I did not want to be alone, ever.

Sarah's nemesis

I had a dream the other night about Morgan, Emily's sister's cat. The cat, as you will see, is the great nemesis in my life. I dreamed about the time Emily's sister, Barbara, was visiting us. Morgan, who had no use for me, would lie on a wooden, four-legged captain's chair in the living room and every time I passed underneath, faster than that cat could blink, she would swat me in the head with her paw. On this particular day, George was sitting in the living room watching television while I was snuggled between his left leg and the arm of his lazy boy. Morgan came slithering up to the lazy boy, stared at George and then leaped onto his lap. I looked up at Morgan and she glared down at me. We were eye-ball to eye-ball with her standing on George's lap and me on his left side. Now, I know people fix cats, and it was my guess that Morgan was in a pretty good position to fix George. I'm thinking, "if I make the wrong move, George and I are both in trouble."

Remember now, when Emily found me at the animal shelter she was looking for a Persian Siamese cat for her sister. Well, we can forget that. Morgan was no Persian Siamese. She was a huge, Himalayan lynx. And, the only time I ever heard the word lynx was when I overheard Emily telling George that she saw a large lynx that had no tail in the big cat section of our local zoo. No wonder I was always spooked when I looked Morgan in the eyes.

Anyway, as I was saying, Morgan was standing on George's leg and I was unpleasantly conspicuous where I was.

When I looked up into those enormous, spooky sky blue eyes of Morgan's, I could swear I saw a sign inside that said, "Don't mess with this cat, sucker." But, hey! I wasn't going to be intimidated. So, to show her a thing or two, I put my head down, stretched out and pretended as though I was back sleeping. Seeing that I was no longer a CATastrophic threat to her, she moved from George's lap and positioned herself between his right leg and the arm of his chair, leaving us in an intensely precarious position. There was no way that I could get up and go without George and I feeling the wrath of Morgan's Freddie Kruger-like claws.

When I glanced up at her with only one eye half open, Morgan caught me feigning sleep. She was just standing there glaring at me. Then she did something I hadn't expected. She nonchalantly turned, slid off the chair and onto the floor and trotted away (sigh). I thought how lucky George was to have escaped with his privates intact and how lucky I was to have gotten away without receiving a frontal lobotomy.

A short time later here came Morgan sneaking back. Sure enough, she jumped on George's lap and the same scenario took place. However, this time George left nothing to chance. He put Morgan on the floor, rose from the chair and left the room. He had had enough excitement for one day. I stayed where I was and Morgan navigated north by northwest back to the captain's chair.

Speaking of cats in the captain's chair, I recall another close call. Like all youngsters, I thought I could get away with anything. One evening Emily was sitting on the living room couch sipping a hot drink. As she left to wash her hair, she put her mug on the arm of the couch to cool. While she was gone I noticed her drink and thought I'd better check it out. I jumped to the couch and performed my nose test. Whatever was in that cup sure smelled good. Since my nose test proved tantalizing, I decided to try my taste test and, likewise, my taste test proved to be enjoyable, very enjoyable; before I knew it, I had reached the bottom of the cup. Whoops!

Worried that Emily would suspect it was me who consumed her drink I decided to hide behind the couch. However, my jump to the floor was not the most graceful I have ever performed. I looked like someone who had just dived from a diving board and with both arms and legs extended to her sides, and belly flopped on the carpet. I tried to walk away, but I had a difficult time standing, let alone walking. When Emily returned she saw me stumbling around the room with chocolate all over my face. Then she noticed the empty cup sitting on the arm of the couch; the cat was out of the bag! Emily went to the telephone and called my veterinarian. He told her that since I was only an 8 pound dog, a cup of hot chocolate mixed with a shot of Captain Morgan's Rum could be fatal. Most certainly I was drunk. Say what? The vet told Emily that I would probably sleep a lot and to watch me closely. Emily was terrified. As for me, I was sick as a dog! From that day forward, anytime I saw a cup within reach, I would give it my nose test and if it smelled of chocolate, I passed up the opportunity to indulge.

Since I have admitted to a drinking problem I might as well own up to one of the great fears of my life. No, it isn't Morgan. It started in the middle of the summer, when I really enjoyed being outdoors. It was so frightening, though, I always wanted to go inside immediately, and hide. Usually it began with a loud bang or I would hear a high screeching, whistle-like-sound that would start at one end of our neighborhood and end up at another.

These noises and bright flashing lights continued well into the night. On occasion, when I couldn't get into the house fast enough, I actually would see this terrible monster as it went screeching brightly through the sky. Even though each sound lasted only a few seconds, it caused my heart to pound, my ears to ring and, often, left me sneezing. All of the noises and flashes created a nightmare for me. Bang, bang, bang, boom, boom, boom, zoom, zonk, crash, bang. It was so bad. If you've ever seen that old Batman television series, you know what I mean. After each explosion, a nauseous cloud would float in the air and the smell would drive me crazy. I was so frightened. I only hoped none of my animal friends knew how frightened I was during those July summer days. I just knew I was the only animal alive that feared fireworks.

Now, I'm sure you have picked up on the fact that my fear is in the past. Credit goes to George and Emily for that. They helped me get over my fear of fireworks. After the first couple of years of seeing me traumatized from exposure to loud sounds and bright, flashing lights, George and Emily did not leave me at home alone and they did not sedate me. Instead, they would drive me to Liberty Park for the annual Fourth of July fireworks display. As soon as the program started, George and Emily would take turns holding me ever so close to them, making me feel safe from the real world and the world of fireworks. As rockets went screeching upward into the night's sky, George and Emily would stroke my head and speak softly, assuring me that everything was okay and that they loved me. In the safety of their arms I finally saw bright, colorful, star-like particles burst into small fragments and fall gently, silently into the dark. Because they took the time and had the patience to see me through these trying times, I no longer feared rockets, fire crackers, sparklers and the like.

Approximately five years ago, our household grew from three to five. George's and Emily's fathers moved in with us when they grew too old to care for themselves. Now, I had two more companions to play ball with. I had always loved using tennis balls when I played catch with George because they were soft and didn't hurt my mouth. George had a lot of balls! He played tennis five days a week and after each match he placed the used balls in a cardboard box in the hallway. When he wanted to work on his serve or other parts of his game, he transferred them to his tennis bag and went to the park and practiced. When I wanted to play ball I just helped myself. Emily was always complaining that I had balls all over the house. Like George, I needed all those balls to keep in practice.

Having George's and Emily's fathers move in gave me the opportunity to share some of my recreational activities. Boy, were they surprised when they saw how great I was. There were three games of ball that I specialized in, and one that I was especially spectacular. In that game, someone would roll the ball along the ground and I had to catch it before it stopped. At home, I caught most balls before they hit the wall because I could get exceptionally good traction on the carpet. When I was younger I was really quick on my paws.

My next favorite game was having someone toss the ball into the air for me to catch. It didn't count if it hit the ground first; I had to catch it before it bounced. Sometimes I would leap up and, twisting my body in an ungodly way, I would make the big catch. I was goood. The last of my three games is what Emily and George called "monkey in the middle." Weird! All the time we played that game, I never saw any monkeys; there were only the three of us there. Anyway, the way we played this game was Emily and George would sit on the floor, facing each other, while I stood in the middle and . . . ? ? ?   Monkey in the middle!   Nooo wayyy.

I've digressed. Let me get back to talking about Emily's and George's fathers. Emily's father lived with us for five years, George's father two. There were times when both were sick and our attention had to turn to their needs. My job was to be cute, keep quiet, stay out from under their feet and provide comfort. Piece of cake.

On several occasions, both fathers suffered strokes and each had to go to the hospital and then to a rehabilitation center for a couple of weeks. At different times, of course. That's when I got to help with their therapy. George and Em would sneak me in their rooms, put me on their good side and have them reach to pet me from their bad side. How could they resist reaching for me? I was their friend too. This ploy worked wonders and soon we were all home again.

The last time Emily's father came home from the hospital was the hardest. He never did get better. There sure was a lot of commotion. A special bed with bars on it was brought into the living room and lots of people were going in and out daily. One day, when it was quiet and no one but Emily was sitting with her father, I dug deep and jumped to the chair by his bed (by then I was 16 years old in people years, no spring pup). From there I sprang to the bed. Emily's father was on his side. I couldn't see his face, only his back. I sat there for a minute, cocking my head from side to side, waiting for him to reach for me as he always did for his therapy, but he made no attempt. I sniffed around him, but he still didn't try to pet me. Leaning up against him I felt his body twitch. I waited for his hand, but no hand moved. His body was just twitching. Not understanding completely what was happening, I felt my ball-throwing friend drifting away, and I was sad. I curled and laid against his back and he seemed to relax. The next day my friend died.

I was lucky to have met him, and I was proud to have been able to comfort him in his last days. I missed him.

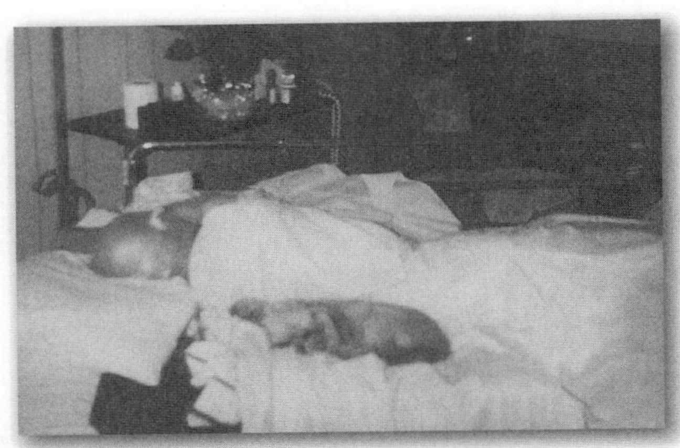

In the last few years I have heard George and Emily refer to me as Pacer instead of Shadow.

I have to admit I do pace throughout the house a lot, but then I always did, usually as Emily's shadow. The difference now is, I cannot control myself. I continually pace from room to room and I always follow the same path. And, I'm no longer following Emily. From Shadow to Pacer to Perpetual Motion, no longer able to see clearly, hear or smell, the path is my reminder and comforter. For as long as I am alive, I don't ever want to forget my home. I don't want to forget those I've shared it with either. It has been such a wonderful life.

The past five or six days have been very tough. I'm sleeping about 22 hours a day. For the short time that I'm awake, I go outside, where the light hurts my eyes, only to use the potty. I eat and drink. Nothing more. Because my eyesight is obscured by thick cataracts, I only see shadows; I hear even less than I see. Sitting is a struggle and falling is a problem. I'm so tired all the time that I do nothing but sleep. I dream, and I remember. In my dreams I have such wonderful visions of playing with Emily and George. I'm running, fishing, chasing a ball and doing other fun things. I dream about when I first came to live with them and of all the great places we went and the happy things we did as a family. Nevertheless, now it's time for my life's journey to end.

CHAPTER V

A world-without-end

By Friday, May 8, 1998, Sarah had not eaten for three days nor taken much water. She was not feeling well. We took Sarah to the veterinarian to see what could be done for our little girl. After examining her, the doctor told us there was not much. Even though she appeared to be constipated, the doctor said she was void of food. He believed Sarah's kidneys were probably failing and to be sure, he would need to do a number of tests. Because of her age and physical condition, he said, we might want to consider putting her to sleep. Tears slid down our cheeks as we realized that we were being asked to make a decision we didn't want to make. The doctor said he could give her a shot that might help with her vomiting. He assured us, however, she would not get better. We asked for the shot and said we would make our decision tomorrow. This would give us the opportunity to say good-bye, and be with Sarah one last night.

We spent the entire evening sitting on our front porch telling Sarah how much we loved and enjoyed her. We reminded her of the fun places we had gone and the things we had done and how she always made us smile. Because we were told there was nothing the doctor could do to improve the quality of her life, we struggled with the dilemma of whether we should have the tests run or have her euthanized. Some friends and family felt we had already kept her a year longer than we should have. We didn't think so, and even at that moment, we still weren't ready to let go. We went to our bedroom, placed Sarah on her pillow, said "Good night precious, we love you." Then we went to bed, wondering what the next day would bring.

The following morning when Sarah got up, she headed straight for her day-old dog food. Emily hustled to the cupboard and quickly opened a fresh can for Sarah's dish; she put fresh water in Sarah's bowl. We were pleasantly surprised as Sarah ate all of her food and drank most of her water.

Afterward, she went to the living room and fell asleep on her pillow there. She slept most of the day and into the evening. Around 10 p.m., she awakened and decided to go on one of her running sprees. She only ran a few feet before she fell. She got up and tried again but, George grabbed her and held her. She was extremely excited and was fighting to get out of George's hands. She was acting as though she was having some kind of seizure, heart attack, or convulsion. We were scared. We would have taken her to the veterinarian right then, but it was too late. When she finally appeared to be over her ordeal, we took her to our bedroom and placed her on her pillow where she immediately fell asleep. The next morning, because she appeared to be back to "normal," we decided not to take her to the veterinarian. It was not a hard decision to make, because we selfishly still were not ready to let her go. We were determined to hold on for as long as we could. We prayed Sarah would die at home, quietly and comfortably in her sleep, protecting us from our responsibility to have her euthanized.

Sarah slept most of the next nine days. When she wasn't sleeping, she strained to sit and to lie down because of her arthritic legs and back. Walking or running, she constantly struggled to maintain her balance and, eventually, fell. When she needed to potty, we carried her up and down eight cement porch steps to our front yard to prevent her from tumbling down. Sometimes Rasta, a large German Shepherd, unexpectedly would come upon

Sarah while she was trying to potty. Rasta would put her huge wet nose between Sarah's back legs and lift her skyward. Fighting for all she was worth to maintain her balance, Sarah must have wanted to tell Rasta to keep her nose out of Sarah's business. As soon as Sarah finished, she would immediately go back inside and head straight for her pillow. She would circle the pillow until she had it trampled into a comfortable position, and then she would lie down and sleep. She had no interest in other dogs or staying outside to sniff or look around.

Preoccupied with the thought of having Sarah put to sleep, I was hit with a wave of tears. The visualization of Sarah no longer a part of my life became more vivid. I began to pace the floor, wondering if I should call our new parish priest. Perhaps he would ease my pain with some wise, comforting words or sound advice on whether or not we had the right to have Sarah euthanized. Then again, he might think I was crazy to be upset over the death of a dog; that I was being childish, fretting over having her put to sleep. Hopefully, he would be sensitive to my grief over the anticipation of her death.

With hesitation, I dialed the parish number. Through controlled sobs, Father listened quietly as I explained Sarah's situation. To my relief, he did not think I was being foolish, his response was "As Sarah's friends, we needed to help end her suffering. Unlike our human friends," he continued, "whom, because of their souls, we do not have the right to help." Not sure I understood, I asked if he meant there was no dog heaven. With a firm conviction, he said, "Dogs do not go to heaven or anywhere. They have no souls." Having said this, he then sympathetically offered to accompany George and me to the veterinarian's clinic when the time was right for having Sarah put to sleep.

I wanted to end our conversation right then. My Sarah has the most gentle and loving spirit and I could not deal with the idea that it would cease to exist when and if we decided to have her put to sleep. I thanked Father for his time and support, hung up the phone and just sat there. How could he know? Even if he didn't, just by his raising the question of soulessness to me, he pushed me deeper into depression.

Stunned by the words of our priest, I could not understand how God could let my flawed spirit live on and Sarah's die. I started to recall taking Sarah to be blessed on the feast day of St. Francis. It was a crisp Fall day and the church yard was filled with people and their pets. There were hamsters and iguanas as well as numerous cats and dogs. We each came to celebrate and to ask for God's blessing on our pet. I remember when Sarah received her blessing. There was a peaceful feeling that came over me as the priest prayed and sprinkled her with holy water. By doing this ritual, the priest publicly recognized that my loyal and loving Sarah -- my pet -- my friend, was a creation of and a gift from God. The thought of Sarah's spirit dying and having no where to go would make my grieving and the decision to have Sarah euthanized more difficult.

The following Tuesday, May 19, Emily frantically screamed for "GEOORRGGE". George arrived to see Emily sitting on the living room floor holding Sarah's limp body in her arms. George gathered Sarah from Emily's arms and held her tight against his body. Sarah's eyeballs were bulging, her breathing was labored and her little heart thumping wildly. Frightened, Emily said that Sarah had been running in the house when she suddenly fell. Laying on her side with her legs stiffened and head thrown back, Sarah let out the most mournful cry Emily had ever heard or ever wanted to hear again. That left George comforting Emily and Sarah. He was sure that as soon as Sarah calmed down all would be right.

While gently stroking her head and talking to her in a soothing voice, Sarah's eyes softened and her look of panic slowly melted away. When Sarah's panting and thumping heart returned to normal, George put her down and watched as she walked steadily to the kitchen and took a drink of water. Afterward, Emily gently cradled Sarah in her arms. Emily and George sat together, stroking Sarah's body, each feeling her pain. Neither wanted to let her go, but both knew what had to be done. Postponing euthanasia was not fair to Sarah, their little girl of seventeen years. Tomorrow would be the day to free her of her pain.

Night came and nobody slept.

Wednesday May 20

While Sarah was still sleeping, Emily made coffee and the two of us had a couple of cups while trying to read the morning newspaper. Neither of us uttered a word. At nine, Emily called the veterinarian's office. To have our dog euthanized we needed to make an appointment. We also wanted a separate cremation for her. (It was our understanding that unless we requested a separate cremation Sarah would be cremated with other dogs and there would be no way of telling which were her ashes.) Sympathetically, Emily was given a 2:30 appointment. Since we had five hours before we had to be at the veterinarian's, we spent some of that time taking pictures. They would be the last pictures ever taken of us together. As time passed, our uncertainty lingered. Could we do it? It was unquestionably the thing to do, but could we do it?

In the past, Sarah would shake uncontrollably whenever she had to go to the veterinarian. Not this day. She was calm and showed no signs of being afraid. At 25 minutes past two, we pulled out of our driveway and drove to the veterinarian's office, only five minutes away. Emily could not hold back her tears as she went to the front desk to report in. I was holding Sarah and, unlike Sarah, I wasn't so brave. I was trying to fight back the tears that clouded my eyes. I didn't want a young lady, who was in the waiting room holding her daughter, to see a grown man crying. But try as I would, the tears did not stop coming. I turned my back, still holding Sarah, walked to the window and stared into space. I tried to block out what I knew had to be done.

It was only minutes before we were directed to an examining room. Colorful wallpaper with cute little puppies dancing and playing decorated the room. Except for two chairs, and a stainless steel examining table in the middle of the floor with a small colorful blanket laying on it, obviously left for Sarah, the room was empty. As we waited for the veterinarian, Emily held Sarah and the two of us continued to speak softly to her.

When he entered the room, the doctor appeared nervous, probably because he could see how emotional we were. He politely asked if we wanted to leave Sarah with him or be with her as he gave the injection. Still unable to control our tears, we told the doctor we would stay. He said he felt obligated to explain the difficulty of finding a good vein in older dogs for injecting the drug. Many times it takes a lot of probing to find one, he said. There can be seizure-like reactions to the overdose of serum and the seizures could be short-term or last up to eight minutes. This could include, but not be limited to, certain spastic reactions, such as head jerking, twitching legs, flinching and other muscle responses. However, the drug he would use was so effective that Sarah would be brain dead and her heart would stop instantaneously. She would feel no pain even though she may appear to suffer. The doctor was concerned that we might be traumatized if we were to witness Sarah having seizures. Reluctantly, but now worried about each other, we told him we would wait in the examining room. The doctor excused himself and left the room.

He returned with a young lady he introduced as his assistant. Then, looking at Sarah, he said, "Sandy, meet Miss Sarah. Miss Sarah, meet Sandy." The doctor lifted Sarah from Emily's care and carefully placed the colorful blanket around her. It was very quiet as the three of them left the room.

Shortly, the door opened and in walked the doctor. He had not been out of the room for more than 30 seconds and, now he was standing before us with Sarah in his arms. Very softly, he said, "It's over. She went very fast and she felt nothing." He laid Sarah on the table still wrapped in her blanket. He told us to take whatever time we needed to say good-bye to Sarah and to let him know when we were ready to leave. Once again, he left us alone.

We couldn't believe she was dead. Looking at her, we felt a sudden void and hopelessness. Because she had experienced so much discomfort over the past month or so, I also felt a sense of relief seeing her so peaceful. She was no longer in pain. As for Emily, she was numb. Numb because it happened so fast. We wish we had stayed with her in those last seconds of her life, and we regret to this day having chosen not to. We believe Sarah has forgiven us.

We spent about fifteen minutes just stroking her body and telling her how much we loved and were going to miss her. When it was time for us to leave, we kissed her little head and walked out of the examining room. Outside, the fresh air seemed to soothe our swollen eyes. On our way home Emily said she wanted to go to her church that evening and pray for Sarah. I asked her to say a few words for me; I wanted to be alone.

Later that evening Emily told me she had asked God to watch over Sarah and to let her know how much we loved and missed her. She thanked Him for the time we had with Miss Sarah's gentle spirit. Because the week had been so emotionally draining, both of us went to bed early, and, exhausted, we cried ourselves to sleep.

CHAPTER VI

The power of storybook reality

On the fifth day following Sarah's death, we walked into the park as two men were removing a bench from the back of a Salt Lake City Parks and Recreation truck and were putting it where Sarah's bench was to be placed. The smaller of the two men returned to the truck, opened the door and waited inside. The other man seemed to be waiting for us. He stood about six feet three or four, was in his mid-forties, slender in build and dressed in blue jeans, a solid blue T-shirt, a Utah Jazz cap and a pair of black Nike running shoes. As we approached him, he smiled and said, "Hi! You're the people responsible for this bench, aren't you?"

Shocked, I said, "Yes, but how did you know?"

With a quizzical stare on his face, he said, "Good question. I have no idea. I just seemed to know. Come to think of it, from the time my partner and I put this bench on our truck, I've had this strange feeling. Tell me, is Miss Sarah a dog?"

"Why do you ask?" Emily quickly responded. He thought for a moment and then motioned for us to join him on the bench.

When he spoke, he seemed to pause

between every few words as he said, "You know,--for some reason--I just knew--Miss Sarah was a dog." Emily looked at me and I at her; not saying a word, the two of us just grinned.

Emily and I spent approximately fifteen minutes telling our story to this man and he listened to every word and when we finished, he asked, "Do you want to hear something really bizarre?" Without waiting for an answer, he continued, "Three weeks ago my pet of eleven years was run over by a car and my wife and I have had a tough time accepting her death." With the side of his first finger of his right hand, he removed a small but noticeable tear that was trying to free itself from his right eye. No sooner had he pushed it away, more followed.

He cleared his throat and continued, "I take full responsibility for what happened. I had only left her unattended for a moment, a moment I will never forget. Our little terrier somehow got off her leash and being somewhat disoriented, walked into the street. She had poor eye sight and probably didn't see the car coming." He told us that he and his wife have a difficult time sleeping and his wife cries a lot. The two of them have not been able to cope with their loss. He thought about getting another dog but he didn't think it was a good idea just yet and it was possible that he might never want another one.

His lips suddenly turned into a smile, as he said, "Today, when my partner and I picked up your bench, I had this feeling that something good was going to happen and it did. I met you two and you know -- it's strange how free from guilt I now feel. It's almost as though a healing spirit has mended my broken heart. Having heard your story about Sarah, I believe strongly that she's here with us right now." He stood, shook our hands and as he turned to leave, he said, "Thank you for sharing your story and . . . Oh yes, thank Sarah for me."

"You're welcome and we will. And, thank you for sharing your story with us," Emily responded.

As we watched him walk away neither of us said another word. We were too stunned at this man's story and the transformation in him from tears to laughter. Emily and I were left sitting there convinced, as was our new friend, that Sarah was watching over the three of us as we traded stories. We were certain she could hear every word and see every move we made. We believed that this kind man, who had lost his four-legged friend of eleven years, was the first to be touched by Sarah's new comforting power.

Today, we have only to go to the park and sit on Sarah's bench to feel our hearts lifted. We feel her presence as we sit and remember great vacations, special moments and the love we had for one another. The void we have gradually disappears, replaced with tender memories and our knowing that Sarah is at peace with God. Yes! Dogs Have Souls Too.

Now faith is the substance of things hoped for,

the evidence of things not seen.

HEBREWS 11: 1

Gone with the Wind -- August 11, 1999

A tornado swept through Salt Lake City's Memory Grove park snapping or uprooting every last tree that has matured since planting started in the park after World War I. With spirits dampened, but not destroyed, nearly 500 volunteers converged on their park to clear and replant.

The spirit never dies.

ABOUT THE AUTHORS

George and Emily Watson are graduates of the University of Utah's Gerontology Program and former State Certified Long-term Care Ombudsman with the Salt Lake County Aging Services. They speak to a variety of social, religious and professional organizations on pertinent aspects of the challenges and choices in elder care.

The Watsons' interest concerning person to person relationships in late life and end of life care issues, led them to write THE CALLING -- A Journey on the Path of Parent Care, ISBN 1-8 8 8 1 0 6 - 9 0 - 5. Their interest in person to pet relationships inspired them to write DOGS HAVE SOULS TOO -- The Spirit of Miss Sarah.

CONTACT THE AUTHORS

Readers of this book are encouraged to contact the authors with comments and stories for their future book.

George and Emily Watson
1012 Garfield Avenue
Salt Lake City, Utah 84105

Web site: http:// www.dogshavesouls.com
Email: sarah@dogshavesouls.com